UPDOG

THE BEST OF
GAMING

WOMEN IN GAMING

Laura Hamilton Waxman

Lerner Publications • Minne

Lerner Publications Company
An imprint of Lerner Publishing Group, Inc.
241 First Avenue North
Minneapolis, MN 55401 USA

For reading levels and more information, look up this title at www.lernerbooks.com.

Main body text set in ITC Franklin Gothic Std.
Typeface provided by Adobe Systems.

Designer: Viet Chu

Library of Congress Cataloging-in-Publication Data

Names: Waxman, Laura Hamilton, author.
Title: Women in gaming / Laura Hamilton Waxman.
Description: Minneapolis, MN, USA : Lerner Publications, 2021. | Series: The
   best of gaming (UpDog Books) | Includes bibliographical references and index. |
   Audience: Ages 8–13 | Audience: Grades 2–3 | Summary: "Gaming used to be
   dominated by men, but some of the world's most popular streamers and eSports
   players are women. Meet some of the women superstars of gaming and learn
   how they reached the top"— Provided by publisher.
Identifiers: LCCN 2019047604 (print) | LCCN 2019047605 (ebook) |
   ISBN 9781541590496 (lib. bdg.) | ISBN 9781728414119 (pbk.) |
   ISBN 9781728401225 (eb pdf)
Subjects: LCSH: Women video gamers—Juvenile literature. | Women video game
   designers—Interviews. | Video gamers—Juvenile literature. | Video game
   designers—Interviews. | Video games—Juvenile literature.
Classification: LCC GV1469.3 .W4684 2021 (print) | LCC GV1469.3 (ebook) |
   DDC 794.8—dc23

LC record available at https://lccn.loc.gov/2019047604
LC ebook record available at https://lccn.loc.gov/2019047605

Manufactured in the United States of America
1-47568-48098-2/11/2020

Table of Contents

Women at the Top

In 2018, gamer Sasha "Scarlett" Hostyn made history.

http://www ...ement stream and timetables

Twitter:
twitter.com/epiclan

Facebook:
facebook.com/epiclan

Staff | Help
Area | Desk

Steam:

She became the first woman to win a major *StarCraft II* event.

Women gamers such as Hostyn are taking esports by storm.

esports: video games played in contests

Other women are famous game creators.

UP NEXT!
THE SUPERSTARS
OF GAMING.

Famous Women Gamers

Katherine "Mystik" Gunn loved comic books and games. She became a pro *Halo* player.

Gamer Tips: *Halo*

➤ Take time to study the maps.

➤ Pay attention to where your teammates are on the map. Try to stick close to at least one teammate.

➤ Learn when to jump, sprint, crouch, and slide.

➤ Hide behind rocks or in high spots.

Jessica Estephan loves *Magic: The Gathering*. She worked hard to master the trading card game.

In 2018, Estephan became the first woman to win a pro *Magic* event. She went on to join a pro *Magic* league.

league: a group of teams that compete against one another

BIO BREAK!

Name: Kim "Geguri" Se-yeon
Age: 19
Home country: South Korea
Claim to fame: top pro *Overwatch* player

Name: Jessica Estephan
Age: 24
Home country: Australia
Claim to fame: first woman to win a pro
Magic: The Gathering event

Name: Wang "BaiZe" Xinyu
Home country: China
Claim to fame: one of the world's best *Hearthstone*
players

Name: Shauna Wolf Narciso
Home country: United States
Claim to fame: helps create tabletop games
   such as *Dungeons & Dragons*

Name: Jaime Bickford
Age: 26
Home country: United States
Claim to fame: earned thousands of
   dollars playing *Rocket League*

Name: Jane McGonigal
Age: 41
Home country: United States
Claim to fame: created the video game
   SuperBetter to help people feel better

Janet "XChocoBars" Rose plays MMO games such as *League of Legends* and *Fortnite*.

MMO: an online game many people play together. MMO stands for "massively multiplayer online."

Her gaming skills have won
her thousands of fans.

UP NEXT!
CREATING GAMES
WE LOVE.

Awesome Game Makers

Rieko Kodama is a video game artist and producer.

producer: the leader of a team that creates video games

She was one of the first women to work in the gaming industry. She helped create games such as *Phantasy Star*.

industry: businesses that make a similar product, such as video games

Bonnie Ross helped create the *Halo* franchise.

franchise: a series of related games and other products

She became a leader of the
company that sells *Halo* games.

Tracy Fullerton is a video game designer. She runs a school for making and studying video games.

designer: a person who creates and carries out plans for a project

Fullerton is one of many women leading the industry. Together, women players and makers are taking over the gaming world.

Glossary

designer: a person who creates and carries out plans for a project

esports: video games played by pro gamers

franchise: a series of related games and other products

industry: businesses that make a similar product, such as video games

league: a group of teams that compete against one another

MMO: an online game played together by many people. MMO stands for "massively multiplayer online."

producer: the leader of a team that creates video games

Check It Out!

Carmichael, L. E. *How Do Video Games Work?* Minneapolis: Lerner Publications, 2016. How do video games work? What are the parts inside a game console? Read this book to find out!

Ellenport, Craig. *Esports: A Billion Eyeballs and Growing.* Broomall, PA: Mason Crest, 2018. Learn about the growing popularity of the esports industry.

Esports Earnings
https://www.esportsearnings.com/players/female-players
Check out this list to see the top-earning women in esports.

Online Gaming Tips for Kids, Teens and Tweens
https://staysafeonline.org/resource/stop-think-connect-online
-gaming-tips-kids-teens-tweens/
Stay safe while gaming with these tips.

Owings, Lisa. *The World of Esports.* Minneapolis: Lerner Publications, 2021. Read about the biggest events and prizes in the world of pro gaming.

Top 20 Richest Female Gamers in Esports
https://www.gamedesigning.org/gaming/female-gamers/
Learn more about the women of pro gaming.

Index

Photo Acknowledgments

Image credits: Leon Neal/Getty Images, p. 4; © ESL Gaming, pp. 5, 6; Rob Monk/Edge Magazine/Future/Getty Images, p. 7; Gabriel L. Guerrero/Shutterstock.com, p. 8; rafastockbr/Shutterstock.com, p. 10; Dorann Weber/Getty Images, p. 11; Mindy Best/Getty Images, p. 13; JOHANNES EISELE/AFP/Getty Images, pp. 14, 15; © GDC, p. 16; Kiyoshi Ota/Getty Images, p. 17; ROBYN BECK/AFP/Getty Images, p. 18; MARK RALSTON/AFP/Getty Images, p. 19; Fred Hayes/WireImage/Getty Images, p. 20; Gonzalo Arroyo Moreno/Stringer/Getty Images, p. 21. Design elements: Nusha777/iStock/Getty Images; cundra/iStock/Getty Images.

Cover image: Earl Mcgehee/WireImage/Getty Images.